CONTENTS

OVERVIEW

Members of the cast are gathered to invite everyone to listen to their story. It is the greatest story ever told, which took place long ago, but is still remembered many years later.

Song 1   TWO THOUSAND YEARS AGO

The angels are excited. The Chief Angel has received news of a very special party, and has to set about inviting the guests on the list. The first guests are Mary and Joseph who accept their invitation. A census is arranged to get them on their way to Bethlehem!

Song 2   BUMPY JOURNEY

Aching and tired, Mary, Joseph and the donkey arrive in Bethlehem to find it crowded, busy and over-booked. One innkeeper who is hosting a Census Party offers them a stable.

Song 3   NO ACCOMMODATION

Next on the guest list is a bunch of shepherds who prove a little difficult to wake! Angel 'Foghorn Fred' is called in to deliver their invitation.

Song 4   THERE WERE SHEPHERDS

The shepherds hear the good news and set off eagerly to go and meet the newborn King.

Song 5   HEY, HO, AWAY WE GO!

As they reach the stable, all is still and quiet. They tiptoe in to hear Mary singing a lullaby.

Song 6   GO TO SLEEP

The angels have to find a suitable way of inviting the three wise men who are on the guest list. What better way of distracting them from their studies than with a Superstar!

Song 7   WISE MEN

All kinds of guests are now gathered for the birthday party of all time! The choice of venue, however, seems rather unusual…

Song 8   IN A STABLE

The angels check through their guest list - it seems to go on for ever! Everybody, past and present - audience included - is now invited to join in the celebrations. (…Party on!)

Song 9   IT'S A PARTY!

Bring out the party poppers, streamers etc, and have yourselves a <u>very</u> happy Christmas!

CAST LIST AND SUGGESTED PROPS

CHARACTERS

Narrators* (7 if possible)	Donkey
Chief Angel	Shepherds* (minimum 4 speaking)
Angel Foghorn Fred	Three wise men
Angels* (speaking and non-speaking)	Sheep* (minimum 1 speaking)
Mary	Innkeepers/Crowd* (non-speaking)
Joseph	Dove
Census Man	Star

*denotes flexibility in numbers - to suit your requirements

SUGGESTED PROPS

Golden note for Dove
Very long guest list (computer paper)
'Angel 1st Class' sash
Map of Galilee
Sewing/broom for Mary
Carpenters tool for Joseph
Bell for Census man
Letter for Mary and Joseph
2 x Banners:

> "CENSUS PARTY, TICKETS 100,000 SHEKELS, FIRST COME, FIRST SERVED"

> "BIRTHDAY PARTY, ENTRANCE FREE! ALL WELCOME!"

Megaphone
Gifts for Wise Men marked Gold, Frankincense, Myrrh
Toy sheep for shepherds to bring

COSTUMES

All costumes should be traditional, with the exception of the Narrators, who should be dressed in the colours of the rainbow. Animals can be dressed in relevant colours with their faces painted, or with masks. The Star could wear a large golden cut-out, or even be dressed as a 'pop star'.

SCRIPT

There are several narrators dressed in bright colours. The angels need to be on an upper level, if possible. The text marked 'Angel' can be shared out as desired. The angels could have a distinctive way of moving from one level to the other e.g. strike 'Superman' pose and skip then jump to indicate arrival.

NARRATOR(S)   Welcome to our story, it's one you just might know,
It happened once upon a time, two thousand years ago!

Song 1. *TWO THOUSAND YEARS AGO*

NARRATOR   It happened in a stable, which wasn't very clean,
Who could guess that it would be the **greatest** party ever seen!
(Enter Chief Angel and other angels. Enter dove).

NARRATOR   One day a snow-white dove brought a golden note,
From God to his chief angel, who cheered…

CHIEF ANGEL   Yes!!!

NARRATOR   …then cleared his throat. *(CA shows long guest list)*

CHIEF ANGEL   There's going to be a party, and we've got to sort out the invitations!

ANGELS   What sort of party? Will we get cake? Can I have a party bag? etc.
(Chief angel waits for silence – teacher style!)

CHIEF ANGEL   This party will be different – but really cool! Come here and I'll tell you about it!   *(The angels gather round and they freeze)*

NARRATOR   The party was a birthday one, but a party like no other
It was for Jesus, God's own son, *(Angels unfreeze)*

CHIEF ANGEL   I must invite his mother!

Angels put on him 'Angel 1ˢᵗ class' sash. Some fetch a large map marked Galilee and point out to him Mary's house.Mary enters on lower level and CA flies to her and jumps to indicate landing! They mime Mary being told God's plan.

NARRATOR   So he invited Mary to be mother of God's son
She didn't worry what to wear, but said…

MARY   God's will be done! *(exit CA).* Joseph! Joseph! *(He enters)*

MARY	You'll never guess what's happened! *(She whispers, he faints, Mary catches him)*
CHIEF ANGEL	*(Back on upper level with angels)* The party is to be in Bethlehem. How can we get them there? *(All freeze, thinking. CA has idea. Child comes on carrying light bulb card! He claps. Census man appears).*
CENSUS MAN	*(Ringing a bell)* Hear ye! Hear ye! Census in Bethlehem! Your country needs YOU! *(He gives letter to Joseph)*
JOSEPH	*(Reading)* We'll have to go Mary, but it won't be easy!
NARRATOR	They couldn't take a taxi, a car or bus or plane, They only had a donkey, so the journey was a pain!

Song 2. *BUMPY JOURNEY*

MARY & DONKEY	Oh my poor back!
JOSEPH	Never mind! I'm sure we'll soon find somewhere to stay.

Lots of people begin to crowd the stage. During next song M & J mime going to various doors, knocking - Innkeepers shake heads at them. During last verse they settle in stable.

Song 3. *NO ACCOMMODATION*

A banner is hung reading 'CENSUS PARTY, TICKETS ONLY 100,000 SHEKELS. FIRST COME, FIRST SERVED'

CHIEF ANGEL	Phew! The first guests are in place! Who's next? Ah yes, the shepherds.
ANGEL	Should be easy peasy japaneasy! *(Enter shepherds and sheep)*
NARRATOR	Oh no…
NARRATOR	It wouldn't be so simple, the shepherds were asleep, They snored <u>so</u> very loudly, they gave earplugs to their sheep! *(They sleep and snore!)*
SHEEP	I'm so tired! Even counting shepherds doesn't help!
CHIEF ANGEL	I'm afraid this calls for a special talent. Call …Foghorn Fred!
ANGEL	That's a good idea! He could even wake up………………! *(Insert name of caretaker/teacher etc)*

Enter Angel Foghorn Fred, possibly carrying megaphone. He takes invite from CA and 'flies' to shepherds, accompanied by lots of other angels.

FOGHORN   *(Very loudly)* Good evening Beth-le-hem! Wakey, wakey! Have I got news for you! *(Opens invite)*

Song 4. THERE WERE SHEPHERDS

At end of song shepherds get ready to leave happily.

NARRATOR   The snoring stopped, the sheep were glad *(Give high fives)*
                      Now they could get some sleep.
                      The shepherds ran off, full of joy, they had a date to keep!

SHEPHERD 1   Come on lads!

Song 5. HEY, HO, AWAY WE GO!

SHEPHERD 1   *(Approaches)* It's very quiet! Maybe the baby's asleep. Let's tiptoe.

SHEPHERD 2   He can't be asleep. I can't hear any snoring!

SHEPHERD 3   Not everybody snores like you!

SHEPHERD 2   *(Taking this as a compliment)* Oh, thanks!

Song 6. GO TO SLEEP

The shepherds slip quietly into the stable.

CHIEF ANGEL   It is going well! We've got a group of three next. *(Enter 3 wise men)*

NARRATOR   The three wise men were busy,
                     Their noses in a book, *(latest Harry Potter)*
                     This invite must be Supercool, to make them want to look!

CHIEF ANGEL   Hmm, *(Thinking)* Supercool, superbright… *(Has idea)* Superstar!
                     (Enter Star, looking like cool pop star)

Song 7. WISE MEN

(During the song they mime spotting the star, who could whistle or call to get their attention, travelling and arriving.)

KING 1   Gold

KING 2	Frankincense
KING 3	Myrrh
NARRATOR	All kinds of guests were present for the party of all time, But there were no balloons, no cake…
NARRATOR	…and certainly no wine (for the grown-ups)!
NARRATOR	Each guest had brought a present, as much as he was able To show how much he loved this baby King born in a stable.
NARRATOR	This King born in a stable, in a tatty, dirty stall Is a King who wants the world to know he came to love us all!
NARRATOR	You wonder why a stable, but it isn't all that odd You don't have to be special to be valuable to God!

Song 8. IN A STABLE

After song the banner is changed to one reading 'BIRTHDAY PARTY. ALL WELCOME. FREE!' CA unfolds list which is excessively long! Perhaps roll of computer paper.

ANGEL	How come there's still such a long list?
CHIEF ANGEL	I told you this party would be a bit different! Everyone's invited - from the year 0 to infinity and beyond!
ANGEL	That's a lot of people!
CHIEF ANGEL	It is! And some of them are here today! *(Points to audience)*
NARRATOR	The shepherds and the wise men got their invites and they came, To see the new born baby King…
NARRATOR	…today it's just the same!
ANGEL	The invite's there for <u>everyone</u> to come and meet the king!
ANGEL	He loves us all and that gives us …
ALL ANGELS	…a great excuse to sing!
FOGHORN FRED	*(To audience)* Come on everybody! On your feet! Let's boogie!

Song 9. IT'S A PARTY!

TWO THOUSAND YEARS AGO

Words & Music by
MARK and HELEN JOHNSON

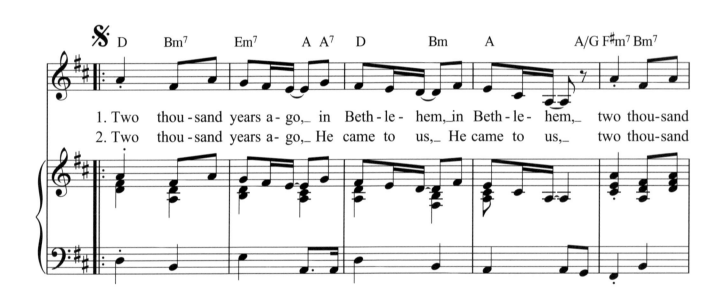

1. Two thou-sand years a-go,_ in Beth-le-hem, in Beth-le-hem,_ two thou-sand
2. Two thou-sand years a-go,_ He came to us,_ He came to us,_ two thou-sand

Chorus

years a-go_ a ba-by King was born. *repeat v.1* Ga-ther round_ and li-sten to our
years a-go_ He came to love us all. *repeat v.2*

Christ - mas sto - ry, though you've heard it ma - ny times be - fore;

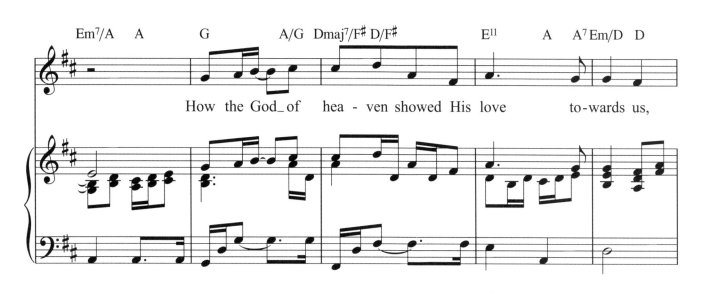

How the God of hea - ven showed His love to-wards us,

so that we can live for e - ver - more!

9

more!

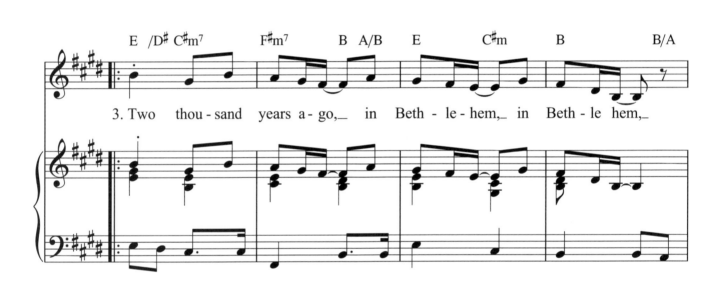

3. Two thou-sand years a-go,__ in Beth - le - hem,__ in Beth - le hem,__

rall. (last time)

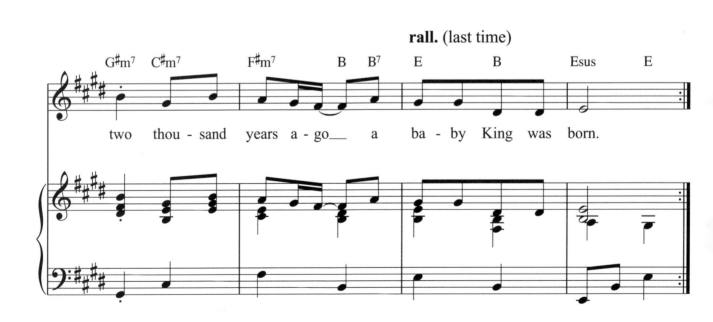

two thou-sand years a-go__ a ba - by King was born.

10

BUMPY JOURNEY

Words & Music by
MARK and HELEN JOHNSON

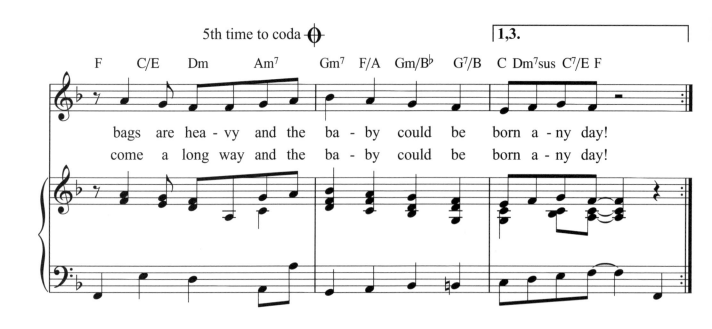

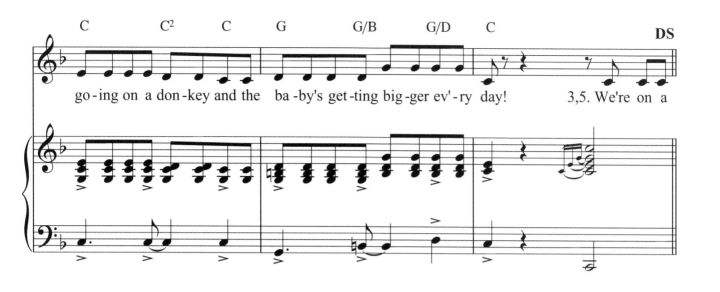

go-ing on a don-key and the ba-by's get-ting big-ger ev'-ry day! 3,5. We're on a

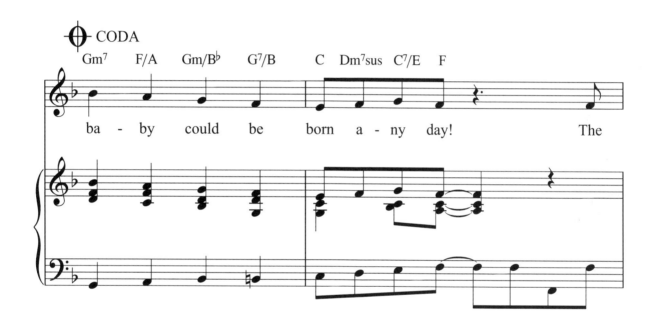

ba - by could be born a - ny day! The

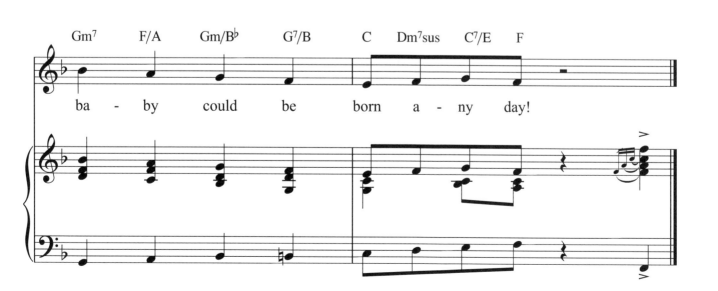

ba - by could be born a - ny day!

NO ACCOMMODATION

Words & Music by
MARK and HELEN JOHNSON

Positively ♩ = 124

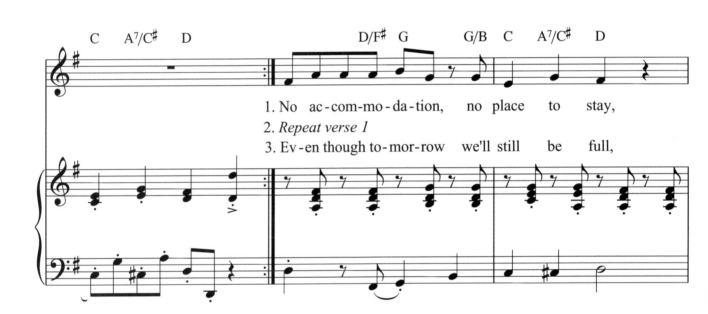

1. No ac-com-mo-da-tion, no place to stay,
2. *Repeat verse 1*
3. Ev-en though to-mor-row we'll still be full,

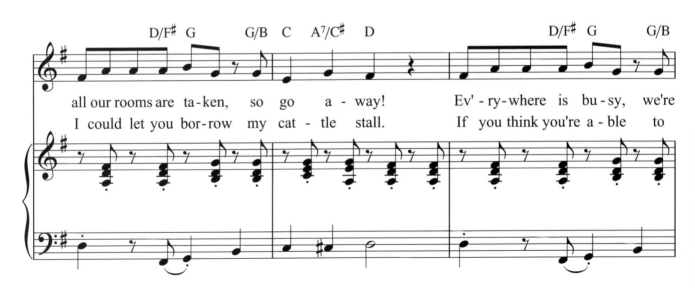

all our rooms are ta-ken, so go a-way! Ev'-ry-where is bu-sy, we're
I could let you bor-row my cat-tle stall. If you think you're a-ble to

14

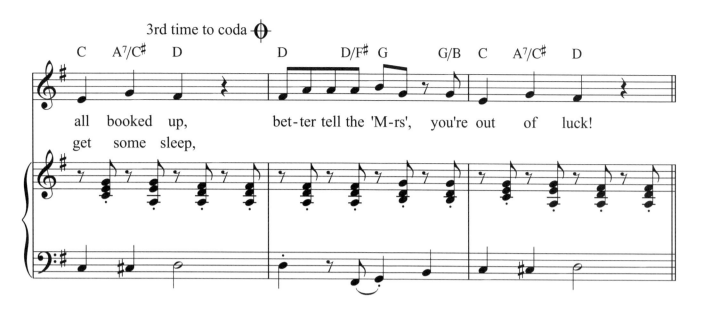

3rd time to coda

all booked up, bet-ter tell the 'M-rs', you're out of luck!
get some sleep,

Chorus

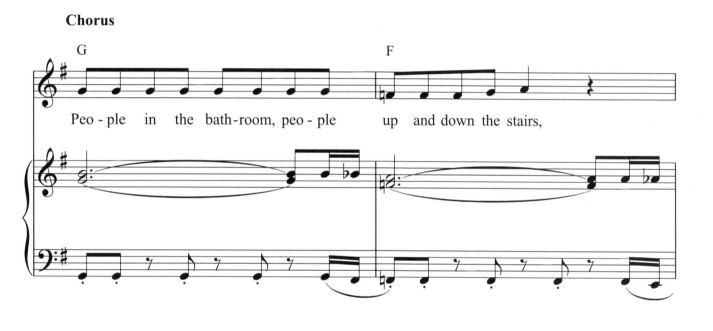

Peo - ple in the bath-room, peo - ple up and down the stairs,

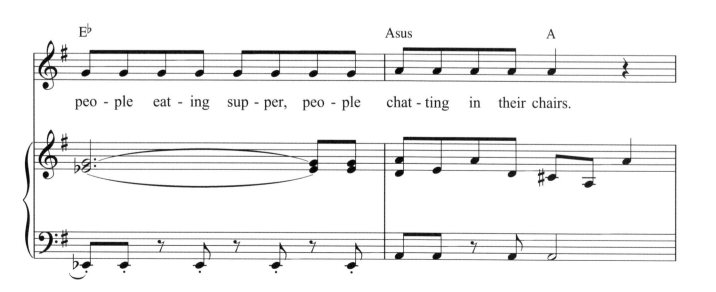

peo - ple eat - ing sup - per, peo - ple chat - ting in their chairs.

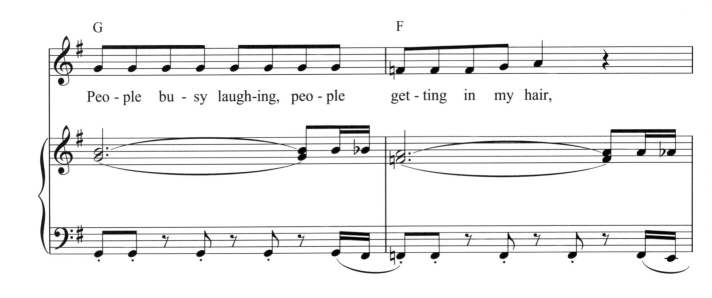

Peo - ple bu - sy laugh-ing, peo - ple get - ting in my hair,

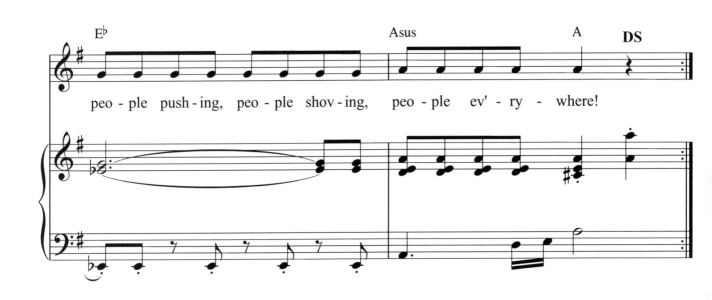

peo - ple push-ing, peo - ple shov - ing, peo - ple ev' - ry - where!

You can use the sta - ble to rest your feet.

THERE WERE SHEPHERDS

Words & Music by
MARK and HELEN JOHNSON

Calypso style   ♩ = 144

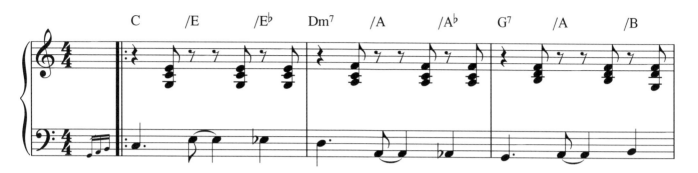

There were shep - herds, liv - ing

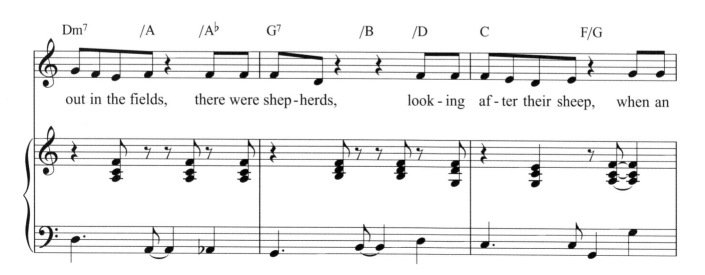

out in the fields, there were shep-herds, look-ing af -ter their sheep, when an

an - gel   did ap - pear in the sky,   and the glo - ry of God__ shone a -

round.   There were round.   And the an - gel   said to the shep-

- herds, "You must - n't be fright - ened, I'm bring - ing you good__ news.   In a

18

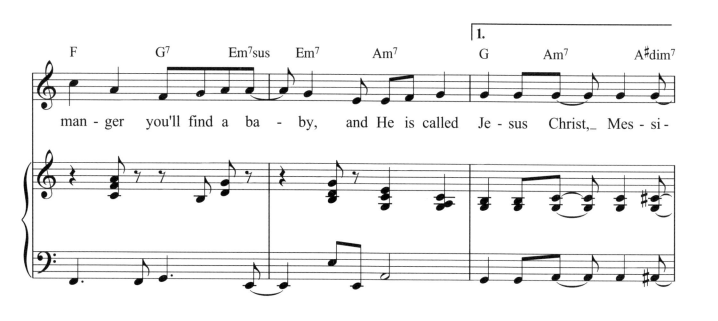

man - ger you'll find a ba - by, and He is called Je - sus Christ,_ Mes - si -

- ah, the Lord!" 2. There were Je - sus Christ,_ Mes - si -

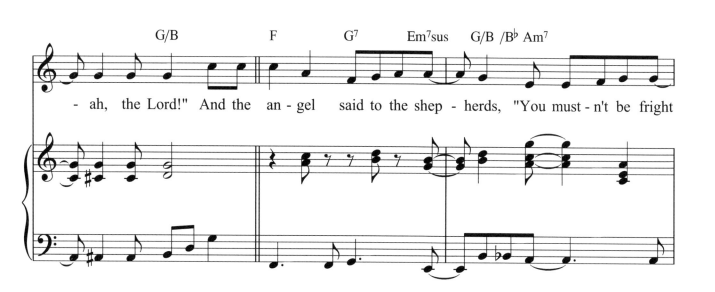

- ah, the Lord!" And the an - gel said to the shep - herds, "You must - n't be fright

-ened, I'm bring-ing you good_news. In a man-ger you'll find a ba-

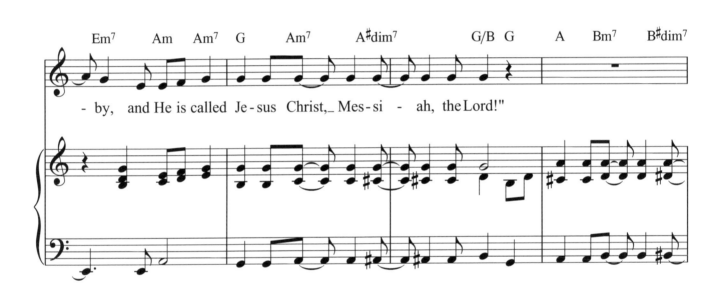

- by, and He is called Je-sus Christ,_ Mes-si - ah, the Lord!"

There were shep-herds, liv-ing out in the fields, there were

HEY, HO, AWAY WE GO!

Words & Music by
MARK and HELEN JOHNSON

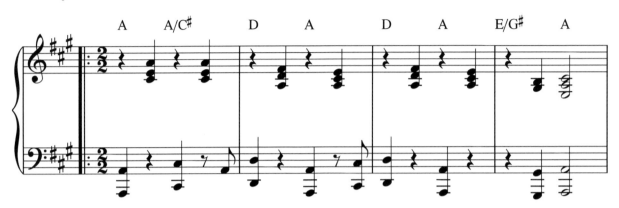

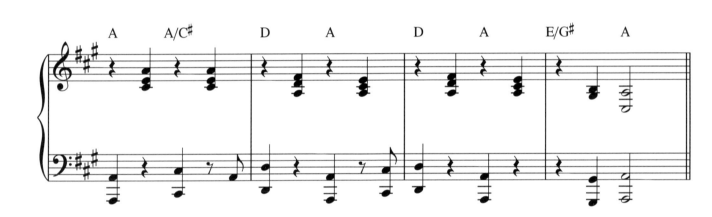

1,2. Hey, ho! A - way we go, we're off to see the ba - by!

3. *Instrumental/dance*

Hey, ho! We've got to go, we'll leave the sheep a - graz - ing.

Chorus

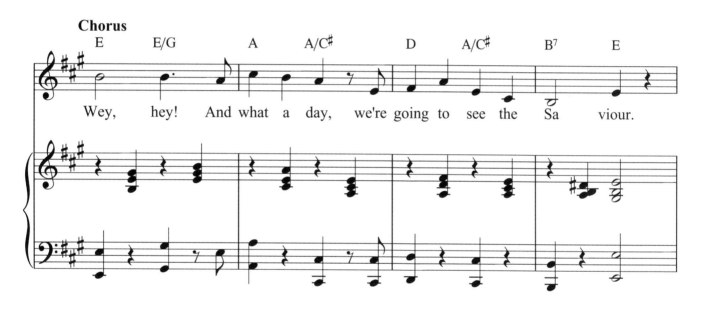

Wey, hey! And what a day, we're going to see the Sa - viour.

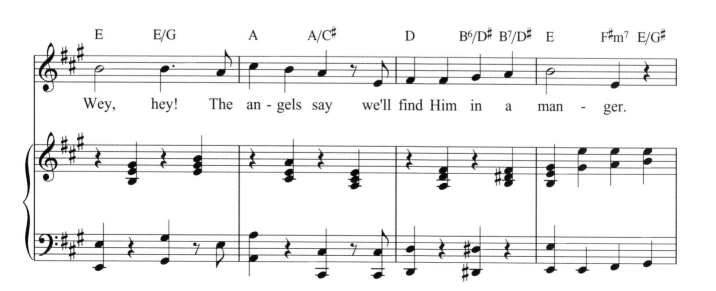

Wey, hey! The an - gels say we'll find Him in a man - ger.

23

GO TO SLEEP

Words & Music by
MARK and HELEN JOHNSON

Smoothly ♩ = 120

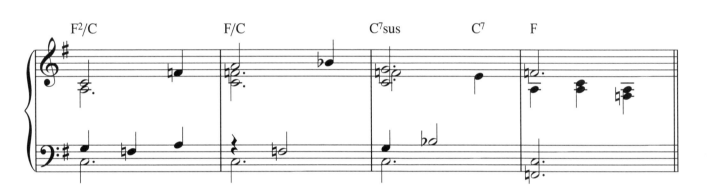

1. Go to sleep, lit - tle one, go to sleep my dar -
2. Go to sleep, lit - tle one, though the night is fal -
3. *Instrumental*
4. Go to sleep, lit - tle one, peace - ful dreams are cal -

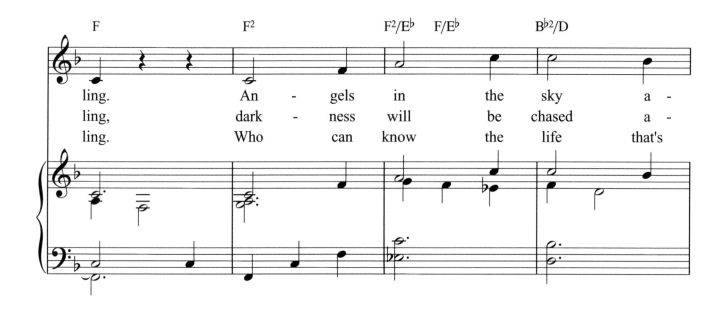

ling.   An - gels   in   the   sky   a -
ling,   dark - ness will   be   chased a -
ling.   Who   can   know   the   life   that's

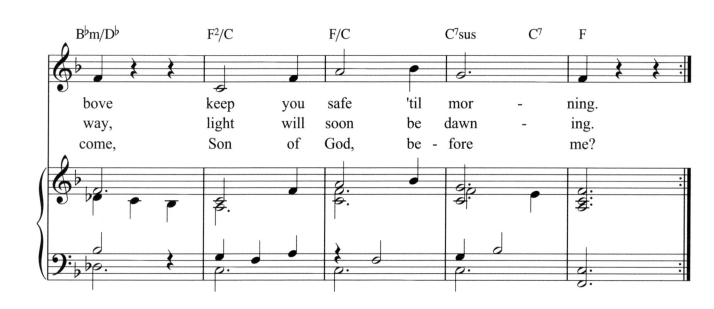

bove   keep   you   safe   'til   mor - ning.
way,   light will   soon   be   dawn - ing.
come,   Son   of   God,   be - fore   me?

WISE MEN
(On a Special Mission)

Words & Music by
MARK and HELEN JOHNSON

With confidence ♩ = 104

1. Wise men,_ wise men,_ came from the East-ern king-dom, rid - ing,_
2. Wise men,_ wise men,_ had seen a new star, it was shi - ning,_
3. Wise men,_ wise men,_ had gone so far and they were tir - ing,_
4. Wise men,_ wise men,_ were o - ver-joyed at last to find Him,_

rid - ing,_ up - on their cam - els._ Wise men,_ wise men,_
shi - ning,_ with such a daz - zle._ Wise men,_ wise men,_
tir - ing,_ from all their tra - vels._ Wise men,_ wise men,_
find Him,_ in - side a sta - ble._ Wise men,_ wise men,_

came from the East-ern king-dom, rid - ing,_ rid - ing,_
had seen a new star, it was shi - ning,_ shi - ning,_
had gone so far and they were tir - ing,_ tir - ing,_
were o - ver-joyed at last to find Him,_ find Him,_

Chorus

up - on their cam - els._
with such a daz - zle._
from all their tra - vels._

Three wise men are

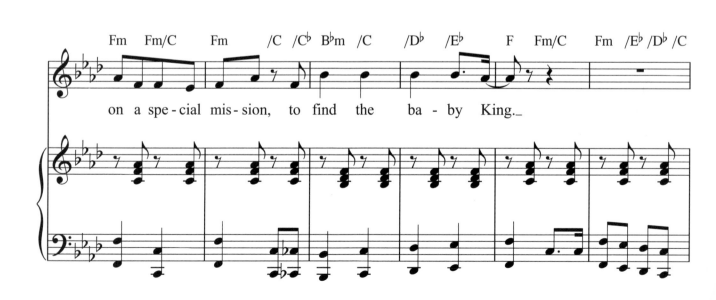

on a spe - cial mis - sion, to find the ba - by King._

28

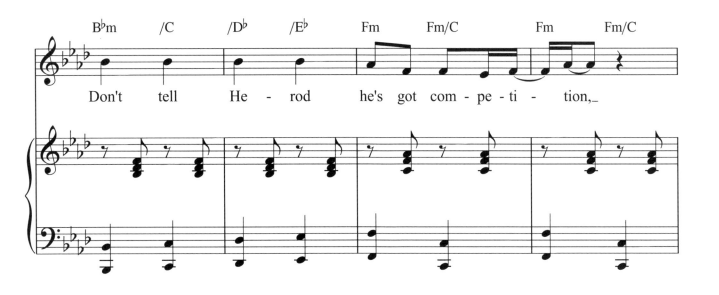

Don't tell He - rod he's got com - pe - ti - tion,

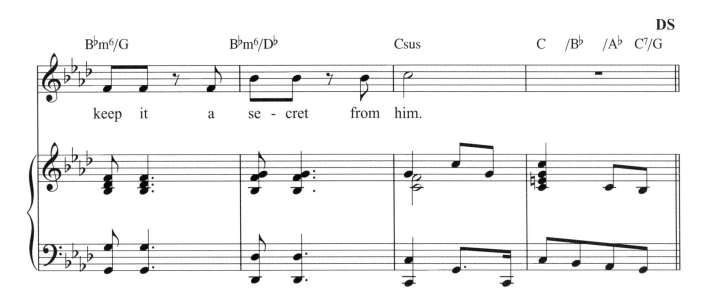

keep it a se - cret from him.

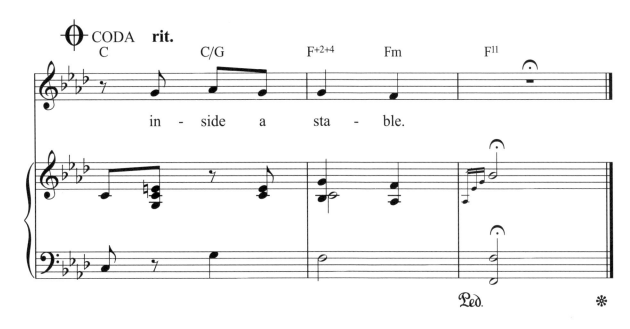

in - side a sta - ble.

29

IN A STABLE

Words & Music by
MARK and HELEN JOHNSON

Reflectively ♩ = 120

1. In a sta - ble long a - go, in a place so far from_
2. Ma - ny an - gels and a___ star, led the peo - ple from a -
3. As we turn our minds a - gain, to the shep - herds and wise_

home, there a ba - by lay whose love would change the world.
-far, to the place where Christ the Sa - viour had been born.
men, and the sta - ble where our sto - ry did be - gin,

And the life that start - ed__ then, on that night in Beth - le -
It was such an awe - some_ sight, to be - hold Him there that_
'though the man - ger now has_ gone, there's a Sa - viour who lives_

hem, would be - come the great - est sto - ry e - ver told.
night, and to know His love would last for e - ver - more.
on, with an in - vi - ta - tion now to wor - ship Him.

31

Chorus

And the an-gels sang at His birth, and His prais-es rang through the earth,

and the skies were filled with songs of wor - ship,

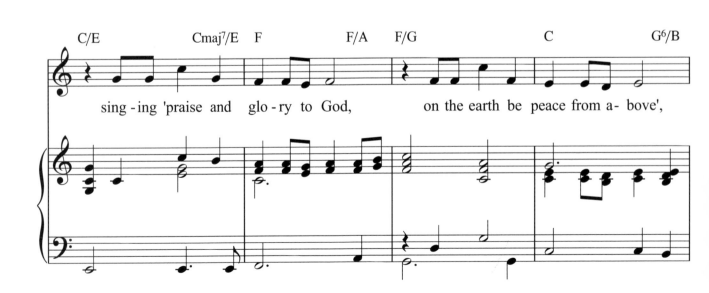

sing-ing 'praise and glo-ry to God, on the earth be peace from a- bove',

for the time had come   for us   to know   Him.

know   Him.

rit.

IT'S A PARTY

Words & Music by
MARK and HELEN JOHNSON

With energy ♩ = 117

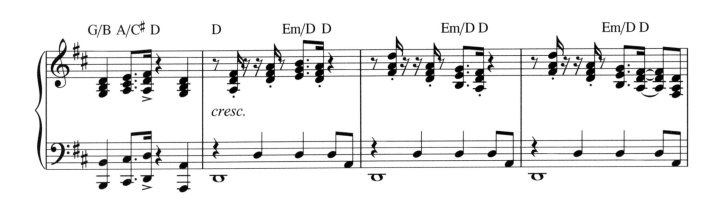

Chorus

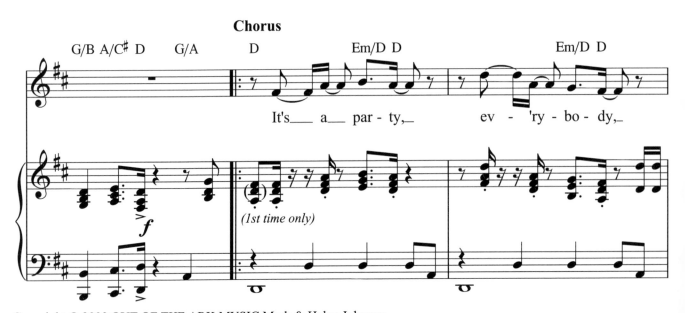

It's__ a__ par - ty,__ ev - 'ry - bo - dy,__

(1st time only)

34

Em/D D   G/B A/C♯ D   Em/D D

it's___ a___ par - ty,___ for ev - 'ry- one!_   It's___ a___ par - ty,_

3rd time to coda

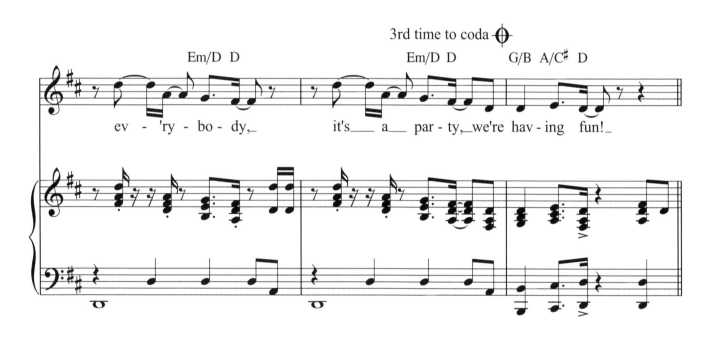

Em/D D   Em/D D   G/B A/C♯ D

ev - 'ry - bo - dy,_   it's___ a___ par - ty,_ we're hav - ing fun!_

A   G D/F♯ G E/G♯   A

1. Je - sus_ the Sav - iour_ has come to us,   -what_ a___ won - der - ful
2. *repeat verse 1*

thing! He is__ Em-man - u - el, God with us,

-He's__ the__ rea - son__ we sing!

hav-ing fun!_ We're sing-ing,_ we're danc-ing,_ 'cause

36

love has_ been gi - ven_ for us to___ know. We're prais- ing,_ we're

laugh - ing,_ with songs of___ re - joi - cing_ a-

round the___ world. We're round the___ world.

Chorus

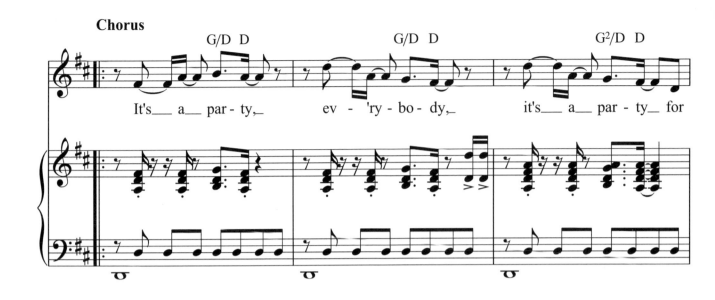

TWO THOUSAND YEARS AGO

1   Two thousand years ago, in Bethlehem, in Bethlehem,
     Two thousand years ago a baby King was born. (Repeat)

     CHORUS   *Gather round and listen to our Christmas story,*
                         Though you've heard it many times before;
                         How the God of heaven showed His love towards us,
                         So that we can live for evermore!

2   Two thousand years ago, He came to us, He came to us,
     Two thousand years ago, He came to love us all. (Repeat)

     CHORUS

3   Two thousand years ago, in Bethlehem, in Bethlehem,
     Two thousand years ago a baby King was born. (Repeat)

BUMPY JOURNEY

1   We're on a bumpy journey
    And we're leaving early,
    Off to Bethlehem and so far away.
    We'll take it nice and steady
    'Cause our bags are heavy
    And the baby could be born any day.
    (Repeat)

    CHORUS   *Got to get a-moving*
              'Cause we're going on a journey
              That'll make us many miles and many ways.
              Gonna have to hurry
              'Cause we're going on a donkey
              And the baby's getting bigger every day!

2   We're on a bumpy journey
    Going very slowly,
    With so far to go and nowhere to stay.
    We're feeling tired and hungry
    'Cause we've come a long way
    And the baby could be born any day!

    CHORUS

3   We're on a bumpy journey
    Going very slowly,
    With so far to go and nowhere to stay.
    We're feeling tired and hungry
    'Cause we've come a long way
    And the baby could be born any day!
    The baby could be born any day!

NO ACCOMMODATION

1   No accommodation, no place to stay,
All our rooms are taken, so go away!
Everywhere is busy, we're all booked up,
Better tell the 'Mrs', you're out of luck!*

        CHORUS   *People in the bathroom, people up and down the stairs,*
                          People eating supper, people chatting in their chairs.
                          People busy laughing, people getting in my hair,
                          People pushing, people shoving, people everywhere!

2   Repeat verse 1

        CHORUS

3   Even though tomorrow we'll still be full,
I could let you borrow my cattle stall.
If you think you're able to get some sleep,
You can use the stable, to rest your feet.

        Alternative line: 'Sorry, it's a pity, you're out of luck!'

THERE WERE SHEPHERDS

1   There were shepherds, living out in the fields,
There were shepherds, looking after their sheep.
When an angel did appear in the sky,
And the glory of God shone around.
(Repeat)

        CHORUS   *And the angel said to the shepherds*
                           "You mustn't be frightened,
                           I'm bringing you good news.
                           In a manger you'll find a baby,
                           And He is called Jesus Christ, Messiah, the Lord!"

2   Repeat verse

    CHORUS TWICE

3   There were shepherds, living out in the fields,
There were shepherds, looking after their sheep.
When an angel did appear in the sky,
And the glory of God shone around.
(Repeat)
And the glory of God shone around.

HEY, HO, AWAY WE GO!

1   Hey, ho! Away we go,
We're off to see the baby!
Hey, ho! We've got to go,
We'll leave the sheep a-grazing.

CHORUS   *Wey, hey! And what a day,*
We're going to see the Saviour.
Wey, hey! The angels say
We'll find Him in a manger.
Hey, ho! Away we go,
We're off to see the baby!

2   Repeat verse 1

CHORUS

3   INSTRUMENTAL/DANCE

CHORUS   *Wey, hey! And what a day,*
We're going to see the Saviour.
Wey, hey! The angels say
We'll find Him in a manger.
Hey, ho! Away we go,
We're off to see the baby!
Hey, ho! Away we go,
We're off to see the baby!

GO TO SLEEP

1   Go to sleep, little one,
      Go to sleep my darling.
      Angels in the sky above
      Keep you safe 'til morning.

2   Go to sleep, little one,
      Though the night is falling,
      Darkness will be chased away,
      Light will soon be dawning.

3   INSTRUMENTAL

4   Go to sleep, little one,
      Peaceful dreams are calling.
      Who can know the life that's come,
      Son of God before me?

WISE MEN
(On A Special Mission)

1   Wise men, wise men,
       Came from the Eastern kingdom,
       Riding, riding,
       Upon their camels.
       (Repeat)

       CHORUS   *Three wise men are on a special mission,*
                       To find the baby King.
                       Don't tell Herod he's got competition,
                       Keep it a secret from him.

2   Wise men, wise men,
       Had seen a new star, it was
       Shining, shining,
       With such a dazzle.
       (Repeat)

       CHORUS

3   Wise men, wise men,
       Had gone so far and they were
       Tiring, tiring,
       From all their travels.
       (Repeat)

       CHORUS

4   Wise men, wise men,
       Were overjoyed at last to
       Find Him, find Him,
       Inside a stable.
       (Repeat)

IN A STABLE

1   In a stable long ago,
     In a place so far from home,
     There a baby lay whose love would change the world.
     And the life that started then,
     On that night in Bethlehem,
     Would become the greatest story ever told.

     CHORUS   *And the angels sang at His birth,*
                    And His praises rang through the earth,
                    And the skies were filled with songs of worship,
                    Singing 'praise and glory to God,
                    On the earth be peace from above',
                    For the time had come for us to know Him.

2   Many angels and a star,
     Led the people from afar,
     To the place where Christ the Saviour had been born.
     It was such an awesome sight,
     To behold Him there that night,
     And to know His love would last for evermore.

     CHORUS

3   As we turn our minds again,
     To the shepherds and wise men,
     And the stable where our story did begin,
     'Though the manger now has gone,
     There's a Saviour who lives on,
     With an invitation now to worship Him.

     CHORUS

IT'S A PARTY!

CHORUS   *It's a party, everybody,*
It's a party, for everyone!
It's a party, everybody,
It's a party, we're having fun!

1   Jesus the Saviour has come to us,
- What a wonderful thing!
He is Emmanuel, God with us,
- He's the reason we sing!

CHORUS

2   Repeat verse 1

CHORUS

We're singing, we're dancing,
'Cause love has been given for us to know.
We're praising, we're laughing,
With songs of rejoicing around the world.
(Repeat)

CHORUS x3

LICENCE APPLICATION FORM

Should you decide to stage one of our musicals, you will need to photocopy and fill in the form below and return it to the publishers, in order to apply for a licence. Licences start from as little as £10 + VAT, depending on your requirements.

APPLICATION FOR A LICENCE

To: **OUT OF THE ARK MUSIC**
        Sefton House
        2 Molesey Road
        Hersham Green, Walton-On-Thames
        Surrey, KT12 4RQ

        Fax: (01932) 703010

We wish to stage (name of musical) **"IT'S A PARTY!" - by Mark and Helen Johnson**	
At (name of school/theatre group):	
On (dates of production):	
Number of public performances	
Total seating capacity of venue	
Expected audience size per performance (excluding pupils)	
Will words to songs be provided in programmes?	
Will admission be charged?	
If so, please give details of ticket prices	
Name of organiser/producer	
Address of school/theatre group	
Postcode	
Daytime telephone number	
Are you recording the show with the intention of selling tapes/videos? YES/NO	
Sound recording YES/NO	No of recordings/copies
Video recording YES/NO	No of recordings/copies